The Park Bench

A Comedy Play

Ashley Burgoyne

Copyright © Ashley Burgoyne 2022

ashleyburgoyne.wixsite.com/writerandcomposer

ashleyburgoynewriter@gmail.com

First Edition published in 2022

Updated in 2023

All rights whatsoever in this play are strictly reserved and applications for permission to perform it, etc., must be made in advance, before rehearsals begin, direct to the author at ashleyburgoynewriter@gmail.com

ISBN: 9798359399456

No one shall make any changes in this title for the purpose of production. No part of this book may be reproduced, stored in a retrieval system, or transmitted in any form, by any means, now known or yet to be invented, including mechanical, electronic, photocopying, recording, videotaping, or otherwise, without the prior written permission of the author. No one shall upload this title, or part of this title, to any social media websites

THE PARK BENCH

First presented at The Little Theatre by the Park, Chesham, Bucks on 1st June 2023 by Phoenix Players Chesham, with the following cast:

Charles	Alex Micallef
Ian	Andy Willment
Stacey	Jen Smyth
Colin	Tony Fraser
Tina	Cathrine Platts
Linda	Jane Dodd
Policeman	Peter Threadgold

Directed by Helen Salisbury

Characters

Charles	70s
Ian	40s
Stacey	20s
Colin	50s
Tina	50s, Colin's wife
Linda	40s, Ian's wife
Policeman	Offstage – voice only

ACT 1

Scene 1

Day 1. Present day. A warm morning in May around 12:00pm. A park. A park bench is in the middle of the stage. Charles enters. He is late 70s/early 80s. He wears a three-piece suit and tie and a thin jacket/mac. He is carrying two shopping bags; one cloth, one plastic. He pauses and stares at the bench for a few moments before sitting down at one end of the bench and placing his shopping bags next to his feet.

CHARLES *(looking directly in front of him)* Glorious, isn't it? *(He pauses and looks up at the sky)* Absolutely glorious! *(He looks down at the mac he's wearing)* Why I listen to them, I don't know. *(Pause)* 6:30 I got up. 6:30 to a glorious blue sky and the man on the radio said clouds with a chance of showers. Chance of showers? *(Looking up)* There isn't even a chance of clouds. Look! *(He points up)* Glorious. *(Lengthy pause. Looking towards the empty end of the bench)* You were right, weren't you. As usual. When it comes to the weather go with your own instinct. That's what you used to say, didn't you, Rose? And here I am, on our bench, overdressed once more. *(Pause. Thinking)* Well. Why change a habit of a lifetime, eh? August 1959, you came and sat next to me, here. Do you remember?

At this point a man and woman come on. They enter from the same side as Charles had. They remain a few steps behind the bench and out of Charles' line of sight. Unknown to Charles (and the audience), they are geocachers. The male geocacher (Colin) is holding a phone. The female (Tina) is holding a pen and compass and they both have rucksacks. They pause. Colin lifts the phone up (to improve the signal), takes a few paces back the way they came, then turns and heads nearer to the bench. Charles continues to be unaware of them as he continues to talk to the empty end of the bench. Tina takes out her mobile phone and quietly takes photos of the bench. They exit the same way as they entered

(Continuing under the above) Boiling hot day and me all dressed to the nines. I'd just been for that interview and had sat myself down here when you, a complete stranger, came and sat there and said "Got enough clothes on, have you"?! Huh! *(Pause. Smiling)* You know, if I'd said that to you, I'd have been arrested!

1

(Pause. Picking up the cloth shopping bag and removing something) I got a lovely chop for tea; look! *(He unwraps and holds a chop towards the empty end of the bench)* I still go to Harold's The Butcher, you know. I mean, it's obviously not Harold any more. Not been him for years.... But they still sell a decent cut. *(He holds up the chop once more before wrapping it and returning it to the bag. Looking in the bag)* Got a few spuds and a tin of pease pudding in there, too. Make a lovely tea that. Mind you; you wouldn't have let me have the pease pudding, would you, Rose? Always green beans with you, wasn't it? *(Pause)* Pease pudding. It's the only thing I have that I never had with you. I do like having the pease pudding. I'd happily get rid of it and go back to the green beans if it meant you being here again.

Pause. A few moments and Ian enters. 40s. He wears a suit and looks a little flustered

IAN *(pointing at the empty end of the bench)* Is this seat taken?

CHARLES Sorry?

IAN This seat. Is it taken?

CHARLES Oh, erm, I suppose it isn't. No.

IAN Ok if I sit here for a moment, then?

CHARLES Er, yes. Fine.

IAN Just it's a bit warm.

CHARLES Yes, it is.

IAN *(indicating both their suits)* And I see I wasn't the only one to overdress today!

CHARLES What? Oh, yes. Quite.

IAN Bloody forecast, eh? When will we learn to ignore it?!

CHARLES My wife said the same.

IAN   Did she?

CHARLES   Yes.

IAN   But, you ignored her and went with the forecast, eh?

CHARLES   Yes.

IAN   She gonna turn up in a minute in a summer dress then, is she?!

CHARLES   She's already here.

IAN   Sorry?

CHARLES   She's already here.

IAN   *(looking around)* Where?

CHARLES   You sat on her.

IAN   *(jumping up)* You what!?

CHARLES   *(laughing)* No, no. I'm sorry. I shouldn't have said that.

IAN   Then why did you?

CHARLES   It's just that that's where she always sat when we came to this park. *(Staring at the empty end of the bench)* She always chose that end of the bench.

IAN   *(still standing)* Oh, I see. *(Pause)* Would you rather I *(gesticulating)* go and you know, erm, find another bench? Leave you two alone?

CHARLES   Two? There's no one else here.

IAN   *I* know no one else's here. I thought that you… *(pointing at the bench)*

CHARLES   What? No. I said that's where she sat. Not that she's sitting there now!

IAN   Oh, right.

CHARLES	I might be old but *(tapping his head)* I'm not cuckoo!
IAN	Right. Of course you're not. Sorry.
CHARLES	No, no. It was all my fault. My silly little joke. Please sit down.
IAN	*(sitting and offering his hand)* Thank you. I'm Ian, by the way.
CHARLES	*(standing and offering his hand)* How do you do, Ian. I'm Charles.

Through the above Ian realises he should stand to shake hands, so, having just sat down he stumbles around to get up again

IAN	*(eventually shaking hands)* How do you do.

Charles sits again. A moment, then Ian follows suit. A pause as both men sit quietly in the sun

	(Reaching into his jacket pocket) Would you excuse me a moment, Charles? *(Pulling out his mobile phone)* I just need to give my wife a quick call.
CHARLES	By all means.
IAN	*(starting to press buttons)* She worries, you see.
CHARLES	Does she?
IAN	*(holding phone to ear)* At lunchtimes.
CHARLES	Oh.
IAN	About where I am. When I'm on my lunchbreak from work.
CHARLES	Really, why's that?
IAN	*(putting his hand up to stop Charles. Into phone)* Hello, love. Sorry I'm a bit late in phoning it's just… no, no love. I am in the park, it's just… no, I don't know where she's gone for lunch, but I'm in the park… who with?

	No one. Just me… I'm late because I started talking to a gentleman… Charles… no I didn't just make that name up! He's here… Alright, I'll put him on *(Charles looks slightly bemused. Cupping the receiver)* Do you mind having a quick word with my wife? I'd really appreciate it.
CHARLES	No, I don't mind.
IAN	Just so she knows that I was talking to you and that's why I phoned late.
CHARLES	*(taking the phone)* Certainly. *(Into phone)* Good afternoon… Yes, I am Charles… No, it's not Dave doing an impression of an old man. My name is Charles and I met Ian a short while ago… In the park… He sat on my wife…

Ian looks towards Charles in disbelief

	Sorry? *(Pause)* She's dead.

Ian puts his head in his hands

	Why would I need to call the police? *(Pause)* No, it was all a bit of a misunderstanding really… Anyway, I'll pass you back now… Nice to have talked to you… Goodbye.
IAN	*(lifting his head and taking the phone with a meek smile)* Thanks.
CHARLES	You're most welcome!
IAN	*(into phone)* Hi, love. Alright... No, no. I didn't kill her… She was already dead! *(Pause)* No, I didn't sit on a dead woman… *(Cupping the receiver. To Charles)* She seems to have got hold of the wrong end of the stick.
CHARLES	Yes. It does seem that way.

IAN   *(into phone)* No, no… look, I'll explain it all when I get home… Yes, ok, I get it. Better a dead woman than her again. Yes… yes, I suppose it does. *(Sighs)* Yes, well, ok. See you later… bye. *(He puts the phone away)*

CHARLES   Alright?

IAN   Erm, yes. I suppose so.

CHARLES   Good.

IAN   Although it would have probably been better if you hadn't mentioned me sitting on your wife.

CHARLES   Really?

IAN   Really.

CHARLES   I just thought it would be better for all concerned if I told the truth.

IAN   Well, yes. I suppose so.

CHARLES   Then there are no little lies to try and keep track of, are there?

IAN   Yes. You're right. Of course. It just became a little complicated.

CHARLES   Did it. Oh dear. What did she say?

IAN   That it all sounded so preposterous that it must be true.

CHARLES   There you go then.

IAN   And that it must also be true as I didn't have the imagination to make up such a story.

CHARLES   Ah. *(Pause)* I did get the feeling, from the part of the conversation I could hear, that maybe this is all of your own doing.

IAN   What is?

CHARLES The fact that you've got an irate wife checking on your whereabouts during your lunchbreak.

IAN Yes, well I suppose it is.

CHARLES There you go.

IAN That obvious, was it?

CHARLES Afraid so.

IAN Ah. *(Pause)* You see it was the office Christmas party.

CHARLES What was?

IAN When I made a mistake.

CHARLES Oh, right. *(Pause)* You don't have to tell me, you know. I mean, we are perfect strangers after all!

IAN Yes, I know. But maybe I need to talk to a perfect stranger. You see; I've only talked to my wife about it. No one else. Naturally.

CHARLES Naturally.

IAN So, would you mind?

CHARLES Mind what?

IAN Mind if I tell you?

CHARLES Well, if it would help you out….

IAN Yes; I think it would.

CHARLES But, I'm no expert. I don't think I'll be able to give you much advice.

IAN Oh, no. I'm not after advice. I think I just need to say it. Get it off my chest. Give myself a chance to move on. Does that make sense?

CHARLES I suppose so. I haven't really had much experience of this sort of thing my –

IAN	*(interjecting)* Great. Thank you, Charles.
CHARLES	Erm, you're welcome.
IAN	I mean it was nothing really. The Christmas party. Usual thing. Stay after work on the 23rd. Party food. Glass of chateau-neuf-du-pape. Usual thing. Know what I mean?
CHARLES	I think I've got the picture.
IAN	One glass followed another. Then the photocopies started going around.
CHARLES	The photocopies?
IAN	Yes, you know; the photocopies.
CHARLES	Photocopies of what?
IAN	*(lowering his voice)* Backsides.
CHARLES	*(unable to hear, leaning forward)* What?
IAN	*(a little louder, pointing down)* Bottoms.
CHARLES	Bottom of what?
IAN	*(looking incredulously)* What? No. Not bottom of anything. Their bottoms. *(Louder)* Bums!

Ian looks around the park to check no one heard him blurt that out!

CHARLES	*(smiling)* Oh, I see. Sorry, Ian. *(Pointing to his ear)* I'm a little mutton in my old age!
IAN	Ah, yes. Sorry.
CHARLES	I'm afraid it comes to us all.
IAN	Yes. I suppose it does.
CHARLES	Carry on.

IAN Yes. *(Regathering his thoughts)* So the photocopies come round and you have to guess whose it is.

CHARLES Whose is what?

IAN *(starting to slightly wish he hadn't started the conversation)* Whose bum is whose!

CHARLES Oh! I see. How interesting.

IAN Well, it is if you've had a few too many *(gesticulating having a drink)* if you know what I mean?

CHARLES Yes. Quite.

IAN Well. The thing is; I don't usually get involved. Department manager, you see. I glance at the odd photocopy as it goes round and drink my wine.

CHARLES Right. What happened this time, then?

IAN I drank too much wine!

CHARLES Ah, I see.

IAN I think I was on about my neuf glass of Chateauneuf, when I agreed to go and… you know.

CHARLES What?

IAN *(gesticulating)* Photocopy my you-know-what!

CHARLES Oh, right.

IAN The problem was, when I went into the photocopy room, someone was already in there.

CHARLES The lady you had your mistake with?

IAN Yes, she's Head of Accounts, you see and it was the first time she'd joined in the game as well.

CHARLES Oh, right.

IAN	And she was in the middle of photocopying when I entered.
CHARLES	I say! What was she doing? Sitting on the machine? I guess that's how you do it if that's the part you're trying to photocopy!
IAN	No; she'd already done that part.
CHARLES	What do you mean?
IAN	I mean that the photocopies of her 'derriere' were sat there in the tray. When I went in she was leaning over doing her... her... *(gesticulating)* breasts!
CHARLES	Good grief!
IAN	And not only that; but she'd not pulled her trousers up from doing her bottom half before starting on her top half!
CHARLES	So she was naked?!
IAN	Almost completely!
CHARLES	*(removing a handkerchief from his pocket and mopping his brow)* Well I never!
IAN	And then, well, then things happened.
CHARLES	Ah, well, yes. I don't think you need to go any further.
IAN	Why not?
CHARLES	Well; I'm a man of many years and I think I know what follows.
IAN	Yes; but it didn't.
CHARLES	What didn't?
IAN	*It* didn't!
CHARLES	*(looking confused)* I'm sorry I'm now a little....

IAN *(looking around before speaking)* We didn't have sex.

CHARLES *(a little taken aback)* Oh, right. Good! *(Pause)* So what's the problem then?

IAN Well; she turned and in her drunken embarrassment she started to apologise and walk towards me.

CHARLES Right.

IAN And it was then that she realised her trousers were still round her ankles.

CHARLES Ah.

IAN She tripped, grabbed all the photocopies of her bum from the tray at the end of the photocopier and fell on to me.

CHARLES Oh my word!

IAN Well, she's quite a big lady, and I was drunk, so I collapsed under her weight!

CHARLES Oh dear, oh dear!

IAN Her lower garments were round her ankles. Her upper garments were round her neck. She was practically naked on top of me and the photocopies of her bum were lying all around us.

CHARLES Well, I never!

IAN The noise we made caused other members of staff to come and see.

CHARLES Ah, at least you were dressed and could explain the situation.

IAN Ah, well, that's where there's a bit of a problem.

CHARLES Why? You were dressed, weren't you?

IAN Yes. Generally.

CHARLES Generally? What does that mean?

IAN Well, you see, the thing was, as I was entering the photocopying room, I'd started to undo my trousers and flies in preparation before I saw her in there. So, as we fell on to the floor my trousers fell down. Not my pants; just my trousers.

CHARLES Right.

IAN So everyone who saw us thought we were, well, at it!

CHARLES Yes, well they would, wouldn't they?

IAN But we weren't!

CHARLES No, of course not. You had your pants on! Didn't anyone see that?

IAN No. No one was interested in the truth. They were all drunk and just found it hilarious.

CHARLES Yes, well, I feel sorry for you.

IAN Well, thank you, Charles.

CHARLES So, what did you do next?

IAN Well, we were both highly embarrassed so we got dressed and went our separate ways.

CHARLES You went home?

IAN Straight away.

CHARLES And told your wife what had happened?

IAN Yes.

CHARLES Straight away?

IAN Well, no.

CHARLES Why not?

IAN It was 2am. Christmas Eve by now. I didn't want to ruin everyone's Christmas, did I?

CHARLES Ah. So, when did you tell her?

IAN The 27th. The day before I returned to work.

CHARLES And she went mad and didn't believe you?

IAN Exactly. She told me if I'd woken her up at 2am and immediately told her she might have believed me, but because I had left it I'd had time to fabricate the story.

CHARLES In what way did she think you'd fabricated the story?

IAN By making sure my pants were on rather than off.

CHARLES Mmm, quite literally fabricating.

IAN Pardon?

CHARLES Oh, nothing. And now you have to report back every day?

IAN Yes.

CHARLES Oh dear, oh dear. Well as I said at the beginning, you should always tell the truth. And immediately!

IAN I know, and that's what I've been doing ever since. But even that's got me into trouble.

CHARLES How come?

IAN A few weeks ago I had to have a meeting with her. You know; department manager and accounts manager. Lots of figures to go over.

CHARLES Right and I suppose your wife queried exactly what figures you were going over?

IAN No. It was worse than that. The meeting was fine, all very professional and so on.

CHARLES Right.

IAN		So I phoned my wife at lunchtime and decided to tell her about the meeting. I didn't have to because it was purely a normal, professional, work meeting, but I thought I would, just to keep things clear.
CHARLES		And?
IAN		Well, she misheard me didn't she.
CHARLES		Oh dear. What did she mishear?
IAN		I told my wife that I'd had a meeting with the accounts manager one to one and that we'd had a maths debate.
CHARLES		A what?
IAN		*(enunciating)* A maths debate.
CHARLES		Ah, yes, well, I can see why she might have misheard you!
IAN		And things have been even worse since.
CHARLES		Oh dear, oh dear.
IAN		And there you have it!
CHARLES		Yes, well, a tricky one indeed. Why would she think you'd tell her… what she thought you'd told her?
IAN		I've no idea. But she wouldn't listen when I tried to explain. *(Pause)* Look, Charles, I know you said you wouldn't be able to give me any advice; but do you have any words of wisdom? Apart from obviously telling the truth.
CHARLES		Immediately.
IAN		Yes, immediately. Even though that seems to backfire on me.
CHARLES		Well, I think it sounds like it's time to move on. Rebuild that trust.
IAN		True. But how?

CHARLES	Well, when was the last time you went out? Just the two of you. Quiet meal, that sort of thing?
IAN	Oh, not since all this happened. Sometime last year probably.
CHARLES	There you go then. Take her out for a meal. Make your peace and suggest you both look forward, rather than back. How does that sound?
IAN	That sounds like a good idea. Thank you, Charles.

Ian offers his hand to Charles. They shake hands

CHARLES	And one more thing.
IAN	What's that?
CHARLES	Speak clearly.
IAN	Oh, right. Yes.
CHARLES	No more maths debating!
IAN	*(smiling)* Yes. Quite!
CHARLES	*(rising)* Yes, well. It's been a pleasure meeting you, Ian.
IAN	*(rising)* The pleasure's been all mine, Charles.
CHARLES	*(shaking hands once more)* I must be off. I have a pork chop in here *(holding up the cloth bag)* which is probably pleading for my fridge by now.
IAN	Oh, right.
CHARLES	Phone your wife now. Go out tonight.
IAN	Right, yes, I will. Thank you, Charles.
CHARLES	Make things right while you can. *(Smiling and looking down at the end of the bench which Ian has just vacated)* Some of us no longer have the opportunity.

Ian joins Charles at staring at the empty bench. Charles quietly turns and exits carrying the cloth bag, but accidently leaves the plastic bag just tucked under the end of the bench. By the time Ian looks up, Charles is gone. Ian goes to sit back down where he was sat before, but thinks better of it and sits where Charles was sitting. He looks at the empty end of the bench for a few more moments and then takes his mobile phone out of his pocket

IAN *(to himself)* Do it now. Go out tonight. That's what Charles said, so that's what I'm going to do. *(He starts to punch numbers into his phone, but then stops)* Maybe I'll just text her. No, no, I can't text her. I'll phone. But what if she doesn't want to go out or worse… she mishears me again! Aah!

He goes quiet whilst fiddling with his phone, apparently texting, but then deleting etc.

Ian's head is down and he only gives a brief look up as the geocachers return. Colin is doing the same as before; looking at his phone and wandering around. Tina, as before, quietly takes photos of the bench, from behind. Ian continues to ignore them. This time they go past the bench and exit the other side.

Ian briefly looks off after them and then briefly looks up when Stacey walks on slowly, from the other side, pushing a pram which has seen better days. She's in her 20s and looks quite exhausted. She's holding a mobile phone to her ear. She stops short of the bench and remains standing whilst talking into her phone

STACEY *(into phone)* I keep telling you Shell, if you go to that club, that's the sort of bloke you're gonna have chattin' you up…. Oh, yeh, you thought this one was different, did you? Why?

Ian looks up during the above comment, then turns his back towards Stacey and plucks up the courage to phone his wife

IAN *(into phone)* Hi love.

STACEY *(into phone)* He said what?

IAN *(into phone)* Alright?

STACEY   *(into phone)* Cheeky bugger! And where was this tattoo?

IAN   *(into phone)* In the park.

STACEY   *(into phone)* Where?

IAN   *(into phone)* The park. Near the ornate lamppost.

STACEY   *(into phone)* Bloody hell! That must've hurt!

IAN   *(into phone)* No, not really. I just thought I'd phone again to try and smooth things over.

STACEY   *(into phone)* So; what was his name?

IAN   *(into phone)* Charles.

STACEY   *(into phone)* Cool name.

IAN   *(into phone)* Dead wife.

STACEY   *(into phone)* Makes a change…. So how old was he?

IAN   *(into phone)* Probably late seventies.

STACEY   *(into phone)* That's not too bad for you. You've had older.

IAN   *(into phone)* He was a really nice man. A proper gentleman.

STACEY   *(into phone)* They all say that. Did you leave with him?

IAN   *(into phone)* No, he had to take his shopping home.

STACEY   *(into phone)* And then what happened?

IAN   *(into phone)* He had to put his warm pork chop in the fridge.

STACEY   *(into phone)* Lucky cow!

IAN	*(into phone)* He really misses his late wife. He used to share this park bench with her and it made me think that I really miss the way we were. Can we start again and look forwards?
STACEY	*(into phone)* How did you do it?
IAN	*(into phone)* Not backwards.
STACEY	*(into phone)* I should think not. Not on a first date, anyway! Then what happened?
IAN	*(into phone)* Dinner?
STACEY	*(into phone)* I usually make sure I get that from them first, Shell.
IAN	*(into phone)* I'll book that little Italian for 8.
STACEY	*(into phone)* Phone number first, Shell, number one rule. Hang on, Shell, his lordship is stirring a bit. I better go.
IAN	*(into phone)* I'll see you later, love.
STACEY	*(into phone)* Catch you later, bye. *(She hangs up and checks on her baby)*
IAN	*(into phone)* Bye. *(He hangs up and puts his phone away)*

Stacey finishes checking on the baby and gets a packet of cigarettes from her small handbag which is tucked in the pram by the baby's feet. She starts to look for her lighter and after a few seconds she gives up looking and sinks on to the vacant end of the bench holding a cigarette. She turns to Ian

STACEY	Excuse me, *(Ian looks up)* do you have a ... *(she waves her cigarette around)*
IAN	Sorry?
STACEY	A, erm, a light?
IAN	Oh, a light. No, I'm afraid I don't smoke.

STACEY Really?!

IAN Yes, really.

STACEY Oh.

IAN You seem to be surprised that I don't smoke,

STACEY Yeh, well I am!

IAN Why? If you don't mind me asking.

STACEY Well, I mean, look at you. *(She waves her hand which is holding the cigarette up and down)*

IAN *(looking at himself)* What about me?

STACEY Well, you're wearing a suit, aren't you?

IAN Yes.

STACEY Which means you probably work in an office.

IAN Yes.

STACEY And you're outside.

IAN Yes.

STACEY Which means you smoke!

IAN Sorry, you've lost me.

STACEY *(sighing)* Men who work in offices only go outside for a smoke.

IAN Oh right.

STACEY You're outside your office and not smoking!

IAN Right, I get you now. No, I'm just outside for my lunchbreak.

STACEY I thought you suited people ate by your computers. That's what I read anyway.

IAN We did once. New Health and Safety rule. Leave the desk before eating lunch. In fact; no food allowed at our desks.

STACEY Right. I get it. *(She puts the cigarette away)* I suppose you think bad of me smoking with a baby. You work for a company with Health and Safety rules and then come across a young mother smoking, well trying to smoke, when she's got a young baby.

IAN Everyone has some sort of vice. I'm sure.

STACEY I never smoked when I was pregnant. I stopped as soon as I found out and I only started again when I stopped breast feeding.

IAN *(feeling slightly awkward)* Well, erm, that sounds like you did very well.

STACEY Sorry?

IAN To stop. You did very well to stop for quite a long time. I believe it's hard to stop.

STACEY Too right. I didn't wanna start again but *(pointing at the baby)* he don't 'alf stress me out. I sometimes need one to relax me.

IAN I see. Hard work, is he?

STACEY Yeh. Trouble sleeping. He likes to be pushed round in the pram to help him get to sleep.

IAN I see.

STACEY He normally nods off within two laps of the park. But, for some reason it took nearly four laps today. I'm knackered!

IAN Oh dear.

STACEY And when it's raining I have to stay in the flat and go round and round the place.

IAN Ah.

STACEY		Not much room in a one bed flat with a pram, you know.
IAN		I guess not.
STACEY		I suppose you've already gone through all this though, haven't you?
IAN		All what?
STACEY		Babies and everything.
IAN		Erm, no.
STACEY		Oh, sorry, didn't mean to assume or pry I just thought….
IAN		Oh, no, don't worry. I suppose most people my age probably have children.
STACEY		Yeh.
IAN		It's just, well…it's just we can't, you see.
STACEY		Oh dear. I'm sorry.
IAN		No, no. We've come to terms with it now. I think. We just don't seem compatible on that front.
STACEY		Ah. And then you see a single mum, moaning about a baby that she never really wanted, not that I'd be without him now, and trying to get a light for her cigarette! What must you think of me?
IAN		You didn't say you were a single mum.
STACEY		Didn't I?
IAN		Must be even harder then?
STACEY		I guess so. Not known it any other way, so don't really know.

Pause

IAN (*pointing at the pram*) What's his name?

STACEY Jim.

IAN Aah. My brother's called James too.

STACEY He's just Jim. Not James.

IAN Oh, I see. You haven't shortened it from James, then?

STACEY No.

IAN Named after the boy's father, is he?

STACEY I told you. I'm a single mum.

IAN Yes; but you still could have named him after his father.

STACEY I wouldn't know.

IAN Wouldn't know what?

STACEY His father's name.

IAN Sorry. I'm afraid you've lost me again.

STACEY I had more than one partner at the time Jim was conceived, so I don't know who the father is.

IAN Oh. *(Pause)* Were any of them called Jim?

STACEY Erm *(pausing for thought)* I don't think so.

IAN Oh.

STACEY There was a John. That was probably the nearest to a Jim. *(Pause)* A Leroy… a Matt… a Dev and a Chris.

IAN *(A little taken aback)* Good gracious!

STACEY It's not as bad as it sounds. You see, I'd been in a long-term relationship which had just ended. So I was making up for lost time; so to speak.

IAN   Oh, right. How long was the long-term relationship?

STACEY   Oh, a good four months!

IAN   Right. *(Pause)* So where did you get the name Jim from then?

STACEY   Ah, well. My waters broke when I was at the cinema with my mate Shell.

IAN   Right.

STACEY   Well, it was terrible. Like the bleeding Niagara Falls it was. Bloke in front thought he was watching a 2D version of the film *(starts laughing)* and he ended up in a very realistic 3D version!

IAN   *(cringing)* Oh dear!

STACEY   Two hours later *(indicating the baby)* out he pops. The midwife hands him to me, having not cleaned him up too well, and I stare down at this little alien and, well, holding an alien having just watched half a Star Trek film I look down at him and blurt out "It's life Jim, but not as we know it" and the midwife says "Jim. What a lovely name" and proceeds to write it down on a soddin' form.

IAN   You could have stopped her. If you had another name in mind.

STACEY   No, well. I didn't really.

IAN   Oh, well. At least you didn't look down at him and say "Live long and prosper"!

STACEY   *(smiling)* Yeh.

Pause

IAN   *(rising)* Look; I need to get back to my desk. Nice talking to you.

STACEY   Yes. You too. Might see you again if it ever takes Jim four laps of the park to doze off again!

IAN	Yes. Bye.
STACEY	Bye.

Ian exits. Stacey checks the baby then bends down to adjust her shoe/do up her shoe lace when she notices the plastic bag under the end of the bench. She picks the bag up and holds it out in the direction Ian exited

Oi, mister! Where's he gone? *(Looking in the bag)* Oh, my! Will you just take a look at that! *(She puts her hand into the bag and pulls out an envelope stuffed full of £20 notes)* What the? *(She flicks through the notes and looks around furtively before returning the money to the plastic bag, and tucking it in the end of the pram. Getting her mobile phone out, she punches a few numbers. She puts her phone to her ear and starts to push the pram)* Shell, listen, you will not believe what I've just found in a plastic bag in the park……

Stacey exits. A moment, or two, and the geocachers return

COLIN	Right. Now let's have a proper look round this bench.
TINA	*(taking photos from behind the bench, as before)* I really don't think it's this bench, Colin.
COLIN	Why not?
TINA	'Coz it doesn't make sense with regards to the clue at all.
COLIN	I don't think any of this person's clues make any sense, Tina. Remember the one over the other side of the park?
TINA	Which one?
COLIN	The one which said it could be found near Victoria Falls.
TINA	Oh, yes.
COLIN	And where was it?
TINA	By the water fountain.

COLIN	Exactly! And not just any water fountain, was it?
TINA	No.
COLIN	No. It was a broken water fountain! Hardly Victoria Falls!
TINA	I think they just have a sense of humour.
COLIN	Maybe they do; but they've no business bringing it into geocaching!
TINA	Really?
COLIN	Really. I want educational clues. Now take another photo of this bench and then we'll try that other one over there *(pointing)*. We can sit on that one and tackle the egg sandwiches *(checking his watch and walking off)*. I think we should start on them soon, as I predict the effectiveness of the cool pack is probably below 50%, meaning that if we don't start on them soon....

Tina takes a few more photos of the bench and follows Colin off stage, whilst shaking her head

Light fades to black out

Scene 2

Day 1. The same, about 45 minutes later. Charles enters.

CHARLES *(muttering to himself as he heads towards the bench)* Retrace your steps, Charles. Don't panic. Well, not yet anyway. Retrace your steps. *(Stopping by the bench)* Now; I sat here and spoke to that man, what was his name? Ah, yes, Ian. That was it. And I put my bags down here *(He points to the side of the bench)* and *(bending down)* nothing there now. *(Pause)* The thing is; did I put the bag down there and then not pick it up? Or did the bag not even make it to the bench? *(Sitting down at his usual end of the bench and addressing the other end as before)* I don't know, Rose. What have I gone and done now? I told you I was going to have that lounge window replaced, didn't I? You know the one. It had lost its seal, or whatever they called it. Just looked constantly covered in condensation to me. So they gave me a quote. I told you the other week. £700. So I thought I'd go and get the money from the building society and pay them in cash when they come next week. I haven't got enough in our current account you see and I know some of these workmen prefer cash, don't they? So I got a thousand out. £700 for the window and the rest for a rainy day. It was in an envelope in a plastic carrier bag and I've gone and lost it. *(Pause. Starting to get a little upset)* I don't know what to do. I just don't know what to do! *(He removes a hanky from his pocket, dabs his eyes and then puts his head in his hands)*

Linda enters, Ian's wife, 40s. She stops short of Charles when she sees he's upset

LINDA *(addressing Charles)* Excuse me? *(No response. Stepping a little closer)* I say, excuse me, but are you alright?

CHARLES *(lifting his head a little)* Mm, sorry?

LINDA I was just wondering if you're ok. *(Pause)* You're not ill, are you?

CHARLES Sorry?

LINDA	*(raising her voice a little)* You're not ill, are you? 'Coz if you are I can call for a doctor or an ambulance, or something….
CHARLES	*(lifting his head more)* What? Oh, no. Sorry my dear. I'm not ill. But thank you for asking.
LINDA	That's quite alright. *(Pause)* Are you sure you're ok? Nothing I can help you with. You seem a little upset.
CHARLES	Yes. I am a little. But I'm afraid there's nothing you can help with. Thank you for your concern. You're very kind.
LINDA	You're welcome. *(Pause)* Sorry if this sounds a little bizarre; but, do I know you?
CHARLES	I don't think so, my dear.
LINDA	*(thinking)* Your voice. I know your voice!
CHARLES	Really?
LINDA	But I don't know *you*!
CHARLES	Well that does now sound a little bizarre as me and my voice do tend to go around together!
LINDA	*(laughing)* Yes, well, I suppose they would.

Charles smiles

	Your name isn't Charles, is it?
CHARLES	*(looking shocked)* My word. It is! How did you know that?
LINDA	Were you sitting here about an hour ago with a man?
CHARLES	Yes, I was.
LINDA	A man called Ian?
CHARLES	Yes. Yes, that was his name.

LINDA *(offering her hand)* Hello. I'm Ian's wife, Linda.

CHARLES *(standing up and shaking hands)* Aah! Linda! Ian's wife. The lady on the phone!

LINDA Yes. The lady on the phone!

CHARLES *(offering Linda the other end of the bench before sitting back down)* My word. You recognised my voice, just from that brief conversation?

LINDA *(sitting)* Yes. And from the fact you're on the bench which Ian referred to.

CHARLES *(looking at the bench)* Ah, yes. The good old bench.

LINDA *(sheepishly)* I'm sorry that you got involved in our little domestic issue, earlier.

CHARLES Not at all. Not at all.

LINDA I didn't realise Ian was happy involving a complete stranger in our domestic troubles.

CHARLES I can assure you he wasn't particularly happy with sharing it; I think he just wanted to try and get a few things off his chest. I just happened to be here!

LINDA Well; I don't know what you said to him, but he's taking me out for a meal tonight.

CHARLES Well, that's lovely.

LINDA Thank you. *(Charles smiles. Pause)* Why are you still here?

CHARLES I beg your pardon?

LINDA Sorry; but Ian said you'd left to go home. Something about putting a pork chop in the fridge I think he said. *(Pause)* I hope he's not lying again.

CHARLES No, no, no my dear. He told you the truth. I did go home and put my shopping away. But I needed to come out again.

LINDA Oh, I see. Well it is a lovely day, so I'm not surprised you decided to come out again. *(Taking in Charles' suit)* Although you do seem a little overdressed for such a nice day. If you don't mind me saying so.

CHARLES Oh, yes. My suit and coat. Funnily enough your husband mentioned that too! No; you see I wasn't going to come out again. It's just that I lost something when I was out this morning, so I've been retracing my steps to try and find it.

LINDA Oh, dear. Nothing too important, I hope?

CHARLES Well, I'm afraid it was rather important actually.

LINDA Oh, dear.

CHARLES It was, well, it was…. Oh, dear! I sound so old and doddery saying this. Which, of course, I'm not!

LINDA Of course you're not. *(Pause)* You don't have to tell me, you know.

CHARLES Oh, no. I don't mind telling you. In fact, it's probably a good idea if I do so that maybe you could let your husband know. He may have found it you see.

LINDA Of course I'll mention it to Ian.

CHARLES It's just so embarrassing.

LINDA I'm sure it can't be that bad.

CHARLES I'm afraid so…. It was an envelope with one thousand pounds in.

LINDA Oh, my!

CHARLES Wrapped up in a plastic bag.

LINDA I see.

CHARLES Not just in the envelope, you see.

LINDA I see.

CHARLES   And I can't remember if I had it with me when I sat down here or not. You see, I may have accidentally left it on the floor next to the bench *(pointing down)*, or I may have just dropped it before, or indeed after, the bench. Although I have retraced my steps this far and I haven't found it since the bench. Or maybe I did drop it between here and home and somebody's taken it.

LINDA   Maybe.

CHARLES   In which case it's probably gone and lost forever.

LINDA   *(trying to cheer him up)* Nonsense. Maybe someone found it and took it to the police station.

CHARLES   *(shaking his head)* Oh, I shouldn't think so. Not a thousand pounds. Not this day and age.

LINDA   Oh, you never know. You should at least try the police station once you've finished retracing your steps.

CHARLES   Yes. I suppose so. Nothing to be lost by trying it. Except my dignity.

LINDA   Oh, don't be so hard on yourself, Charles. People lose things all the time.

CHARLES   Ah, yes, but I don't.

LINDA   Don't what?

CHARLES   Lose things.

LINDA   Oh, I'm sure you have….

CHARLES   No, never.

LINDA   …. at some time….

CHARLES   No.

LINDA   …. lost something?

CHARLES   No.

LINDA Really?

CHARLES Really.

LINDA Nothing?

CHARLES Nothing.

LINDA Not even your car keys?

CHARLES No.

LINDA Oh!

Pause

CHARLES I know it may sound strange, and possibly even big-headed, but I've never lost a thing.

LINDA Well, that's truly amazing!

CHARLES Not really. I just placed everything in its place.

LINDA That's it?

CHARLES Yes.

LINDA Right.

CHARLES I suppose the bag of money didn't have a place, so I don't know where I placed it.

LINDA *(slightly confused)* Yes. That's possible.

CHARLES Once I'd designated a place to place it, then I would have known its place and known where to have found it having placed it in the correct place.

LINDA *(more confused)* Right.

CHARLES But I lost it before I could designate a place to place it, you see.

LINDA Yes....

CHARLES My wife was terrible at losing things, you know.

LINDA Was she really?

CHARLES Oh, yes. She drove me potty with her constant searches for things. I think that's why I made a bit of a fuss over not losing things. I think I over-compensated for her.

LINDA Possibly.

CHARLES And now I haven't just lost a key or a bus pass or suchlike. My first loss is a thousand pounds!

Pause. Stacey re-enters. She is now pushing Jim in a brand-new, expensive looking pram. She stops quite short of the park bench and starts fumbling around in her bag for her mobile phone

LINDA *(glancing at her watch)* Look; I'm ever so sorry, Charles, but I've got a hairdressing appointment I need to keep.

CHARLES Not at all.

LINDA I would stay and help if I could; but when Ian phoned, I thought I'd see if I could get my hair done before our meal tonight and even though my usual salon was fully booked, I found another salon just the other side of the park had just had a cancellation, so I'd better be on time.

CHARLES Of course, of course.

LINDA But I will tell Ian of your predicament.

CHARLES Thank you.

LINDA And maybe I can ask him if he'd meet you here tomorrow lunchtime. Just like you did today. How does that sound?

CHARLES That would be lovely.

LINDA And if you haven't found it by then, maybe he can help you with the next steps.

CHARLES	Thank you, Linda.
LINDA	*(rising)* No problem at all.
CHARLES	*(rising and offering his hand)* It's refreshing to see such helpful young people in this day and age.
LINDA	*(shaking Charles' hand)* Bless you. Bye.
CHARLES	Goodbye.
LINDA	And good luck.
CHARLES	Thank you.

Throughout the above Stacey has found her mobile phone, which she is holding in one hand. With the other she is fussing around Jim; tucking him in etc

LINDA	*(walking past Stacey and glancing into the pram)* Oh, what a darling looking baby!
STACEY	*(pausing from fussing)* Oh, thank you!
LINDA	What's his name?
STACEY	Jim.
LINDA	*(looking into the pram)* Hello, Jim! What a lovely little boy you are and what a lovely pram you have!
STACEY	Thanks! We've only just got it. It's his first time in it.
LINDA	*(into pram)* What a lucky boy you are! *(Standing up. To Stacey)* Cherish every moment. You're very lucky.
STACEY	*(a little taken aback)* Yes, I will.
LINDA	Good. Must dash.

Linda exits. Stacey starts punching numbers into her phone. Throughout the following Charles gets up and exits slowly. He goes past Stacey and the pram, head bowed, as he continues to look for his money

STACEY   Hi, Shell. It's me. Yeh, I got it. The blue. Yeh, had to be really didn't it? You should see it. Lots of chrome and stuff....

CHARLES   *(during the pause in Stacey's phone conversation; just as he passes the pram. To himself)* Bound to be right under my nose. That's what they say. It'll be right under your nose.

Charles exits

STACEY   *(walking off. Into phone)* I tell you what; we'll pop round later and show you it. Unless you're meeting up with that bloke again? No; didn't think you would....

Stacey exits as lights fade to black out

Scene 3

Day 2. The same, the following day, around 12:00pm.
Charles enters. He is wearing less than the previous day; just an open neck shirt and trousers.

CHARLES *(addressing the bench as he approaches it)* No good, Rose. No good. *(Sitting)* I can't find it anywhere. I traced my steps right back to the building society. Even went in, just in case I hadn't picked it up in the first place, but I had…. They even checked the CCTV to show me leaving the premises with the bag. They can't help…. Went to the police station who said that nothing had been handed in. They took my details and gave me a crime number saying they'd get in touch if it's handed in, although they doubt it will be. They're probably right. *(Pause)* I even asked Frank, the postman, if he'd seen it. I don't know why I asked him. Maybe it was because it was in an envelope and him being a postman…. Anyway, the conversation with Frank sort of petered out leaving me feeling quite foolish.

Ian enters. Dressed the same as the previous day. He looks generally happier and less flustered than when we last saw him

IAN Charles!

CHARLES *(rising and offering his hand)* Ian. Good to see you.

IAN *(shaking hands and then sitting)* And you, Charles. Linda told me of your predicament.

CHARLES Ah, yes. All a little unfortunate. Your wife's a charming lady.

IAN Yes. She is, isn't she? Any luck finding your missing money?

CHARLES I'm afraid not, Ian. I was just telling my wife *(gesticulating towards the bench where Ian is sitting)* all about it.

IAN *(looking down slightly awkwardly at the bench)* Oh dear.

CHARLES Mmmm.

IAN And you've retraced your steps?

CHARLES Yes.

IAN And been to the police station?

CHARLES Yes.

IAN Were they much help?

CHARLES No, not really. Not much they can do, I suppose.

IAN Unless there's any CCTV covering the park?

CHARLES There isn't. The desk sergeant said that only the children's play area is covered. Not the rest of the park. Anyway; I don't know whether I arrived here with the bag or not in the first place.

IAN No?

CHARLES No. *(Pause)* Anyway; thank you for coming to try and help.

IAN No problem, Charles. I just wish there was more I can do.

CHARLES Yes. *(Glancing at his watch)* Shouldn't you be phoning your wife? She'll be wondering where you are!

IAN Ah, well, I'm pleased to say that after our meal last night she says I don't need to keep checking in every day.

CHARLES Really?

IAN Yes.

CHARLES That's wonderful.

IAN Thanks to you.

CHARLES Well, I don't know about that. I only made a simple suggestion. That's all.

IAN Yes, but it was the kick start I needed! So, thank you.

CHARLES Not at all. Not at all.

IAN I just wish I could return the favour and help you find your money.

CHARLES I'm afraid that I may have to just accept that as lost and go and withdraw more out of the building society... not that there's much more left.

IAN We can't have that. No. There must be a logical explanation.

CHARLES I suppose so, but I can't find one.

IAN Right; you helped me with a simple suggestion so I'm going to give you a simple suggestion.

CHARLES Right.

IAN Did you stop at all, for any reason, between the building society and this bench?

CHARLES Erm, no.

IAN No other shops.

CHARLES No. I did the butchers before the building society and then set off home.

IAN And you didn't stop for any other reason; like to talk to anyone?

CHARLES No.

IAN Then, unless you dropped it, it made it to this bench where you must have put it down before I met you yesterday.

CHARLES I suppose so.

IAN   Meaning you probably failed to pick it up when you left.

CHARLES   Meaning it was here when you were on your own.

IAN   But I didn't see it.

CHARLES   No.

IAN   But, hang on, I did speak to someone soon after you left.

CHARLES   Did you?

IAN   Yes. A young lady.

CHARLES   Really? What was her name?

IAN   I don't know. She didn't say.

CHARLES   Oh. Shame.

IAN   But, she had a baby with her. In a pram.

CHARLES   *(brightening up a bit)* A young lady with a pram?

IAN   Yes.

CHARLES   A brand-new pram?

IAN   Oh, no. A tatty old thing. Why?

CHARLES   Oh. It's just that I saw a young lady with a pram just after I was speaking to your wife yesterday.

IAN   Really?

CHARLES   Yes. But she had a brand-new pram.

IAN   Oh.

CHARLES   Can't be the same young lady, then.

Pause

IAN Ah.

CHARLES What?

IAN It could be.

CHARLES Could be what?

IAN The same lady.

CHARLES How?

IAN Think about it. I saw her by this bench. In fact, I left her here on her own. She was then seen a short while later with a new pram. Meaning….

CHARLES That she found my money and went and bought a new pram?!

IAN That's what I'm thinking, yes.

CHARLES Surely not.

IAN It's possible.

CHARLES It's possible, yes, but it's also possible that it's a different young lady.

IAN True.

CHARLES We need to be sure before we start making accusations.

IAN Yes.

CHARLES Shame you didn't get her name.

IAN Yes…. Hang on. I didn't get her name, but I did get the baby's!

CHARLES Did you really?

IAN Yes.

CHARLES And what was it?

IAN   Erm. I can't remember.

CHARLES   You can't remember?

IAN   Erm, no.

CHARLES   Oh.

IAN   Damn. I was a bit flustered, having just spoken to Linda on the phone and then the young lady asked for a light, for her cigarette. Then she talked about lunches and the fact that her waters broke at the cinema and that she's a single mum….

CHARLES   You remember all of that, but not the child's name?

IAN   Damn. *(Getting frustrated)* I know! It's stupid.

CHARLES   Retrace the conversation, Ian. In your head.

IAN   Ok.

CHARLES   Calmly.

IAN   Right, yes. *(He sits having an imaginary conversation with an imaginary Stacey. His mouth is repeating words he can remember along with some actions and gesticulations)* Star Wars.

CHARLES   I beg your pardon?

IAN   She was watching a Star Wars film when her waters broke, so she named the baby after one of the characters.

CHARLES   How bizarre!

IAN   Yes.

CHARLES   Which one?

IAN   Sorry?

CHARLES   Which character was the baby named after?

IAN Erm. I can't remember!

CHARLES Oh dear.

IAN Well, it can't be too difficult. Have you seen any of the Star Wars films, Charles?

CHARLES Oh, yes, but quite a while ago. I'm more of a fan of Star Trek.

IAN Really?

CHARLES Yes. I remember watching the original series back in the 60's. Wondrous stuff back then, you know. Before we'd landed on the moon and all that.

IAN Yes. But can you name any characters from Star Wars? Try to jog my memory?

CHARLES Yes, well, there was Luke wasn't there?

IAN It wasn't that. More obscure, I think.

CHARLES Then maybe it was Skywalker?

IAN Not that obscure.

CHARLES No? Anything seems to be deemed a name these days.

IAN Yes.

CHARLES The lady who served me in the building society yesterday was called Tangerine.

IAN Tangerine?

CHARLES Yes

IAN First name or surname?

CHARLES Oh, first name.

IAN I can't begin to imagine what her surname was!

CHARLES Smith!

IAN	Oh, right.... Any more Star Wars names?
CHARLES	Oh yes, erm Leia?
IAN	Oh no, it was definitely a boy's name. I remember that much.
CHARLES	Oh, right.
IAN	Keep listing them, Charles and I'll stop you when I hear it.
CHARLES	Righto! Han...Solo...Darth...Vader...R2, no, not that, erm Obi-Wan...Yoda...Palpatine...Dooku...Jar Jar... Chewbacca?

Throughout the above Ian reacts with increasingly bizarre facial responses to the ridiculous list of names!

IAN	This isn't working, is it?
CHARLES	Not really, no.
IAN	No.

Pause

CHARLES	I've just remembered something!
IAN	What?
CHARLES	I believe your wife may have spoken to the young lady after she left me yesterday.
IAN	Really?
CHARLES	Yes.
IAN	Why didn't you say so?!
CHARLES	Sorry, Ian. I've only just thought of it.

IAN	That's ok. *(Getting his mobile phone out)* I'll call her… *(Into phone)* Hi love…yes, I know you said I didn't need to call, but I'm with Charles in the park… *(cupping the receiver. To Charles)* she says hello… *(Into phone)* I'm trying to help him with his missing money and we believe that both you and I spoke to the same young lady with a pram possibly before and after Charles lost his money… Pardon…? she asked me for a light… that was all… I thought we cleared the air last night…I can't help it if people come and talk to me, can I? Yes, well, can we talk about this later? I'm trying to help Charles at the moment. The lady mentioned her baby's name but we can't remember it. Did she mention it to you? She did? Great! *(Thumbs up to Charles)* It was a long name from Star Wars, wasn't it? Erm… yes. That was it. No, I realise that doesn't come from Star Wars, now… No, it's not a particularly long name either… Right, well, thanks for that, love. See you later. Bye. *(He puts his mobile phone away)* It seems that I got my two sci-fi programmes muddled up.
CHARLES	Oh.
IAN	It was Star *Trek* not Wars.
CHARLES	Right.
IAN	And it wasn't a particularly long, or strange, name either.
CHARLES	Right. What was it, then?
IAN	*(embarrassed)* Erm, it was Jim!
CHARLES	*(laughing)* Jim?!
IAN	Yes.
CHARLES	*(continuing to laugh)* Jim!
IAN	*(starting to chuckle)* Chewbacca!
CHARLES	Jim!
IAN	R2 bleeding D2!

They continue to laugh as lights fade to black out

Scene 4

Day 2. The same. 1pm.
Tina and Colin, the geocachers, are seated on the bench, sharing a flask of tea.

TINA   Better?

COLIN   Hmm?

TINA   The tea.

COLIN   What about it?

TINA   Is it better? Than yesterday's flask?

COLIN   *(taking a sip and swilling it around his mouth)* Yes. Yes, it is.

TINA   Good.

COLIN   That extra half a teaspoon of sugar has made all the difference.

TINA   Good.

COLIN   It's all about ratio. Isn't it?

TINA   And volume.

COLIN   Sorry?

TINA   Volume. As well.

COLIN   Well, yes. Obviously volume, as well. *(Pause)* But mostly ratio. *(Rushing on)* Now; why are we here? Didn't we come to this bench yesterday?

TINA   Yes. Yes, we did. But we skirted around it whilst looking for that other cache.

COLIN   That's right. It had a man sat on it. And then a different man.

TINA Yes. *(She gets her phone out)* I took some photos. Look.

She shows him her phone. Scrolling through a few photos

COLIN Yes. Very good. *(Pointing at a photo)* Although the framing isn't great on this one and the lighting could have been better in that one.

TINA *(looking at the photo)* That's the sun.

COLIN I know it's the sun.

TINA I can't help where the sun is.

COLIN I know you can't help where the sun is.

TINA No.

COLIN But you can help where you are.

TINA What!?

COLIN You can help where you are, can't you? You should have moved to a different position.

TINA What. So that the sun was behind me?

COLIN Yes. That's the idea.

TINA And I was right in front of the bench?

COLIN Exactly!

TINA And right in front of the man.

COLIN What?

TINA If I'd put the sun behind me, I would've been right in front of the man. Probably casting a shadow over him.

COLIN Well. Possibly. Possibly.

TINA Looking a right nincompoop!

COLIN Well, I wouldn't go that far...

TINA *(getting a little annoyed)* You told me the first rule of geocaching was not to look too obvious.

COLIN True. True.

TINA Yet you want me to make sure the sun is behind me when taking photos.

COLIN Ideally, yes. *(Rushing on)* But I fully understand your situation with regards to that photo.

TINA Thank you.

COLIN You're welcome. *(Pause)* That doesn't excuse the framing, though.

TINA *(putting her phone away in disgust)* Really!?

She folds her arms and turns her back towards him. Pause. He eventually pours a cup of tea and offers it in her direction

COLIN Tea?

No response

It's very good. The ratio of sugar to tea... and water... and milk for the volume of the flask is perfect!

TINA *(turning and reluctantly taking the cup)* Sometimes!

They sit in silence for a moment

COLIN So, what did you want to show me in the photos of this bench?

TINA *(retrieving her phone once more and scrolling through photos)* This is the first photo I took of this bench.

COLIN *(looking at the photo on the phone)* Yes.

TINA What do you see?

COLIN The back of an old man sitting on a bench.

TINA	Anything else?
COLIN	No. Although he was the man wittering away to nobody, wasn't he?
TINA	Yes.
COLIN	So he clearly could *see* something, or indeed someone, else. But I can't see anything.
TINA	*(pointing at the photo)* Just there.
COLIN	*(squinting)* Two bags.
TINA	Made of…?
COLIN	Made of!?
TINA	Yes. What do they look like they're made of?
COLIN	*(looking again)* Well… one looks like it's a cloth bag and the other's plastic.
TINA	Right!
COLIN	Oh, good. Do I win a prize, or something?
TINA	*(scrolling through her photos)* Hang on. *(Showing the next photo)* Now what do you see?
COLIN	*(looking at phone)* The back of a middle-aged man sat on a bench.
TINA	*(pointing)* With…?
COLIN	Oh! Just the plastic bag.
TINA	*(showing another photo)* Then, after he left, we returned and I took this photo.
COLIN	*(mystically)* No bag…
TINA	Interesting, isn't it?

COLIN *(in thought)* Interesting… yes. *(Pause)* No. In fact, it's more than that.

TINA More than what?

COLIN More than interesting.

TINA Really!?

COLIN Yes.

TINA Oh. I just thought it was merely an interesting observation, on my part.

COLIN I think we may have stumbled across something, here.

TINA Really!? What?

COLIN A donkey.

TINA *(in disbelief)* A what!?

COLIN The old man. He's a donkey.

TINA *(picking up the flask and sniffing it)* I think I may have actually put too much sugar in here.

COLIN A donkey! A donkey! Can't you see?

TINA I only see an old man. Not a donkey!

COLIN *(sighing)* Not an actual donkey. A drugs donkey.

TINA No. I'm sorry. You're going to have to start from the beginning.

COLIN *(taking her phone)* Old man arrives at bench with two bags. Leaves one behind for the boss…

TINA Boss?

COLIN Younger man. More expensive suit.

TINA Right.

COLIN	Boss sits on bench and nonchalantly picks up plastic bag as he leaves.
TINA	Right.
COLIN	Bag's full of drugs. Or money.
TINA	Is it?
COLIN	Well, I don't know, do I! But that's what it looks like to me.
TINA	Really?
COLIN	Yes.
TINA	Ok. So, where's the donkey come into it?
COLIN	I told you. The old man's the drugs donkey.

Tina is in thought for a little while, then a smile comes across her face. She then, slowly, starts to giggle, which gradually turns into a laugh

	What's funny?
TINA	Donkey!
COLIN	What about it?
TINA	You're the donkey.
COLIN	I beg your pardon!
TINA	It's mule!
COLIN	What?
TINA	It's drugs mule. Not donkey!
COLIN	What? Ah, yes…
TINA	You silly ass!
COLIN	Now, really! There's no need for language like that. It was a perfectly innocent mistake…

TINA   I said ass. As in donkey.

COLIN   Oh, right. I see. An attempt at humour…

TINA   I didn't say a –

COLIN   *(interrupting)* – no. And there's no need to say it now!

TINA   *(muttering)* Donkey…

COLIN   Alright, alright.

TINA   You seriously believe, from my photos, that we've witnessed a drugs transaction.

COLIN   Yes.

TINA   Really?

COLIN   Of course. It's the only logical explanation.

TINA   Well, I don't think it's the only logical ex –

COLIN   *(interjecting. Pointing at the photos)* – you can clearly see they're drug dealers.

TINA   *(looking at the photos)* The only thing you can clearly see is their backs!

COLIN   Even so…

TINA   And what about the young woman with the pram.

COLIN   What young woman?

TINA   You were still fiddling with that water fountain; but I'm sure I saw a young woman, with a pram, talking to the younger man. The boss.

COLIN   Really?

TINA   Yes. I think so.

COLIN   Very interesting. *(Pause)* Pimp!

TINA Sorry!?

COLIN The boss. He's also a pimp.

TINA Now, come on…

COLIN *(picking up the flask etc)* It all makes perfect sense.

TINA Well, it doesn't really. That's just a woman with a baby.

COLIN *(heading off)* Come on. I have a plan.

TINA *(following)* A plan? What do you mean, a plan?

They exit. Lights fade to black out

Act II

Scene 1

Day 3. The same. 11:45am.
Tina and Colin are sat on the bench sharing a bag of crisps.

TINA *(offering an open lunchbox)* Sandwich?

COLIN *(taking one)* Don't mind if I do. Thank you. *(Taking a bite)* Mmm... that's interesting. What is it?

TINA Cajun chicken.

COLIN Sorry?

TINA Cajun chicken.

COLIN *(placing the sandwich back in the lunch box. Quite sternly)* I thought we'd decided.

TINA *(continuing to eat her sandwich)* Decided what?

COLIN The effort I went to with the eggs...

TINA Sorry?

COLIN And the mayonnaise...

TINA Pardon?

COLIN *(pointing at the sandwich)* Then you give me this!

TINA I really have no idea what you're on about!

COLIN *(raising his voice)* Free range! We agreed free range!

TINA Yes...

COLIN Free range eggs. Mayonnaise made with free range eggs.

TINA Yes. And?

COLIN And you give me caged chicken!!

TINA *(quietly opening up the sandwich and showing it)* Cajun.

COLIN *(calming, a little)* What?

TINA Cajun. The chicken is Cajun.

COLIN Oh.

TINA Not caged. Cajun. As in spicy.

COLIN Yes. I know what Cajun means.

TINA Right.

COLIN I just misheard you.

TINA Yes.

Pause

COLIN *(picking up the sandwich)* Sorry.

TINA That's ok.

COLIN *(eating the sandwich)* It's very nice. Thank you.

Pause as sandwiches are consumed in silence

TINA *(taking a plastic bag out of her rucksack)* Is this really going to work?

COLIN I think so. Don't you?

TINA *(removing an envelope of cash from the plastic bag)* Well; the fake cash certainly looks pretty good.

COLIN That 'Geocache for Cash' trail the other year was interesting, wasn't it?

TINA Until the police got involved.

COLIN Well, yes. That was unfortunate.

TINA Yes.

COLIN	I mean, the frenzied increase of geocachers over those few weeks who thought it was genuine cash.
TINA	You did.
COLIN	I did not!
TINA	You did. We went from once a weekend to nightly.
COLIN	Nightly!?
TINA	Yes.
COLIN	You know I've always been just a once a weekend person.
TINA	Yes.
COLIN	Never nightly.
TINA	No. *(Looking away, under her breath)* Don't I know it.
COLIN	Sorry?
TINA	Nothing.
COLIN	At least we were established geocachers and not just jumping on the bandwagon.
TINA	Yes. *(Looking at the cash)* You really should've handed this into the police, though.
COLIN	I know. I just felt, as an established geocacher, that we'd searched for the cache – that's *(spelling it out)* c a c h e – and the *(spelling it out)* c a s h, cash, was ours whether it was real or fake.
TINA	Ok. *(Looking at her watch)* Quickly explain the plan, again.
COLIN	*(taking the bag and placing it by the leg of the bench)* We place the bag here. Just where it was in your photos.
TINA	Yes.

COLIN	*(pointing off stage)* And film the unfolding events from those bushes over there.
TINA	You realise that that's too far away to get any sound.
COLIN	Yes; but there's nowhere else nearer, so pictures without sound will have to do.
TINA	And should we be filming people without their permission?
COLIN	We should if they're up to no good.
TINA	And what are you hoping to see?
COLIN	*(collecting his stuff and rising)* I don't know. Drugs, the prostitute, money exchanging hands... Exciting, isn't it!? *(He exits)*
TINA	*(collecting her stuff and following. Sarcastically)* Positively thrilling! *(She exits)*

Pause

Stacey enters, pushing the new pram. She enters from the opposite end of the bench from where the plastic bag is now situated, by the leg of the bench so there's little chance of her seeing it. She's currently on her mobile phone

STACEY	*(into phone)* He's got what pierced?... And he wants you to pierce the same thing? Well, that's not anatomically possible, is it! Just don't go there, Shell... *(looking into pram and exiting. Into phone)* No, he's still awake. That's three times around. It's going to be one of those days... *(She exits)*

Pause

Ian enters from the same side Stacey entered from. He's currently on his mobile phone, presumably talking to Linda. During the following he sits on the end of the bench away from the money

IAN	*(into phone)* I know I'm seeing you shortly and didn't have to phone, but I wanted to... Well; after last night... I know... When you... Yes... And... Yes... Glad we're not turning into a once a weekend sort of couple... *(He laughs)* No, no. He's not here, yet... I don't really know what to say to him... Yes, ok... Just listen and comfort him... *(At this point Charles enters from the other side. He immediately spots the plastic bag, but stops short of the bench as he's aware of Ian being on the phone)* Ok... Yes; will do... *(he spots Charles and gives a wave. Charles replies with a small wave)* I better go as Charles is here... See you in a bit... Love you... Bye! *(He places his phone in his pocket. Rising and offering his hand)* Charles!

CHARLES	*(smiling whilst shaking Ian's hand)* Ian. How did you do it!?

IAN	*(slightly bemused)* Sorry?

CHARLES	Where did you find it?

IAN	Find what?

CHARLES	*(picking up the bag)* The bag!

IAN	*(looking very confused)* The what!?

CHARLES	*(opening the bag and retrieving the envelope of cash)* The bag! My money!

IAN	*(sitting down and scratching his head)* I didn't.

CHARLES	*(sitting down)* Didn't what?

IAN	Find it.

CHARLES	Then what's this?

IAN	I have no idea.

CHARLES	It wasn't you who put it there?

IAN	No.

CHARLES Oh. When I saw it, I thought you'd put it there as a bit of a joke. You know; as in 'it's been there all the time!' *(He chuckles)*

IAN Erm, no. It wasn't me, Charles. I'd only been here a minute or so, when you arrived. I was on the phone to Linda and hadn't even noticed the bag.

CHARLES Then who else would have known where I'd left the bag, so they could put it back in the correct place?

IAN Well; one person.

CHARLES Who?

IAN The person who took it in the first place.

CHARLES Ah. I see. Then they felt guilty and put it back here?

IAN Maybe. How much is there?

CHARLES Sorry?

IAN The money. Is the full one thousand in there?

CHARLES Oh, I see. *(He starts to flick through the money in the envelope)* Looks a bit short. Around £700, I'd guess.

Stacey enters, pushing the pram a bit slower than before, as she completes her fourth circuit. She's still on the phone. She chuckles occasionally as she listens to, one presumes, Shell

IAN *(nodding towards Stacey)* And how much is a new pram?

CHARLES *(taking in Stacey)* Ah, I see. I don't know. About £300 these days?

IAN That sounds a reasonable figure.

STACEY *(into phone)* I'd get some cream for that. Get on top of it.

Stacey notices Ian and gives a smile and little wave. Ian reciprocates (continuing into phone) That's the fourth circuit, Shell. I think he's starting to look dozy… *(she continues, whilst chuckling, and exits)*

Both Charles and Ian watch in silence as Stacey exits

CHARLES Now what?

IAN I'm not sure.

CHARLES She seemed to remember you, Ian.

IAN Yes.

CHARLES Do you think she'll be coming around again in a few minutes?

IAN I shouldn't think so, Charles. She says that four times is usually enough to get her baby…

CHARLES Jim.

IAN …yes, Jim, to sleep. She was telling the person on the phone that it was the fourth time round.

CHARLES Right.

Pause

IAN What do you want to do, Charles. Report her to the police?

CHARLES I don't think we've got enough evidence for that. Do you?

IAN Not sure.

CHARLES *(looking at the envelope)* I probably have enough here for the window…

IAN Yes.

CHARLES And you said she was a single mum…

IAN	Yes. And she seemed a nice girl, but that's no reason to let her get away with stealing £300.
CHARLES	True. But, as I said, I don't think we've got enough evidence to prove it was her.
IAN	Plus, she was a bit brazen walking past here where the crime was committed.
CHARLES	Maybe it was her way of making sure the money got back to the right person.
IAN	But, she never saw you the other day.
CHARLES	No, but she saw you. Maybe she thinks it's your money?
IAN	Maybe. Anyway, it's your money and it's up to you what happens next, Charles.
CHARLES	*(pondering)* I think I'll leave things as they are.
IAN	Fair enough. *(Looking at his watch and rising)* I should be going.
CHARLES	*(rising and shaking hands)* Ok. Thank you for your help, Ian.
IAN	I didn't really do anything, Charles.
CHARLES	Oh, yes you did.
IAN	Really?
CHARLES	Yes. You made a good impression on that young lady. Making her want to return some of the money, which she must have thought was yours, back to you.
IAN	But not a great enough impression to return all of it!
CHARLES	True. But, if you'd made that big an impression on her, Linda may have had something to say about it!

IAN	*(laughing as he exits)* Never a truer word said in jest! Talking of Linda; I'm meeting her for lunch. I'd better go. Bye, Charles. *(He exits)*
CHARLES	*(laughing)* Bye, Ian. *(Looking in the plastic bag and exiting the opposite way)* Right, Rose. Got it. Well, most of it! Time to designate a place to keep it so I don't lose it again. *(He exits)*

Pause

Tina and Colin return, gingerly, and sit on the bench

TINA	What did you make of that, then?
COLIN	I think we need to upload the footage and watch it on a bigger screen.
TINA	Right.
COLIN	I definitely lip-read the words 'one thousand'.
TINA	Right.
COLIN	And there wasn't that much in there.
TINA	No.
COLIN	Which might have caused tension.
TINA	Possibly.
COLIN	And then the knowing nod and wave between the prostitute and the pimp.
TINA	Yes, I saw that.
COLIN	*(in thought)* Hmmm… yes. *(Standing)* Let's go and study the footage at home.
TINA	*(standing)* Ok.

They exit. Lights fade to black out

Scene 2

Day 3. The same. 12:00pm.
Linda is sat in the middle of the park bench. She's touching up her make up as Stacey enters. Having spoken previously, Linda decides to try and strike up a conversation.

LINDA Hi.

STACEY *(warily)* Hello.

LINDA *(standing and approaching, a little)* Hello. Sorry, but we spoke briefly the other day.

STACEY *(still a little warily)* Did we?

LINDA Yes. I commented on your lovely pram. You told me you'd just got it and that your son's name was Jim.

STACEY *(starting to relax)* Oh, yes. I remember.

LINDA *(looking in the pram)* Ah. Sound asleep.

STACEY I should hope so. Almost five laps of the park. A record I could've done without!

LINDA *(offering the bench)* Have a rest.

STACEY *(manoeuvring the pram to the side of the bench)* Don't mind if I do.

They both sit. Stacey gets out her pack of cigarettes and fumbles for a lighter, like before

LINDA You ok?

STACEY Can't find my bleeding lighter.

LINDA Oh.

STACEY *(holding up her cigarette)* You don't have one, do you.

LINDA Afraid not.

STACEY   (*putting away the cigarette*) Nobody seems to smoke any more.

LINDA   That's surely a good thing, isn't it?

STACEY   I guess so. I wish I could give it up. I did while I was pregnant with Jim; but I find him so stressful at times that I found myself reaching for the cigs again.

LINDA   (*looking into the pram*) He doesn't look like he's stressful.

STACEY   Well, of course he doesn't. He's asleep.

LINDA   I know that…

STACEY   Sorry. I didn't mean to be rude.

LINDA   No, no. Not at all. He just looks so sweet.

STACEY   I suppose he is, really. *(Pause)* Do you have children?

LINDA   I'm afraid not.

STACEY   Oh.

LINDA   My husband and I just don't seem compatible on that front.

STACEY   Sorry?

LINDA   I said that we don't seem compatible on that front.

STACEY   That's bizarre.

LINDA   What is?

STACEY   Those words.

LINDA   What about them?

STACEY   I spoke to a man, right here, just the other day who used those exact words when I asked him if he had children.

LINDA   (*trying, but failing, to sound sincere*) Oh, really?

STACEY	What's going on?
LINDA	Sorry?
STACEY	I said, "what's going on"?
LINDA	I'm not sure what you're getting at.
STACEY	You, saying that, and the man who said it to me a few days ago sitting right here and giving me a wave a few minutes ago. *(Standing up)* Are you the police?
LINDA	*(also rising)* Police!? Of course not.
STACEY	Who are you, then? Who's he?
LINDA	Why would the police be after you?
STACEY	*(slightly cagily)* They're not.
LINDA	Then why say it?
STACEY	I dunno. Just tell me who you both are, or I'll call the police myself.
LINDA	My name's Linda and the man you spoke to was my husband, Ian. He's very fond of telling strangers all of our business!
STACEY	And why was he here only a few minutes ago? Why weren't you together?
LINDA	We're meeting up for lunch. He works near here and I've arranged to meet him. *(Looking at her watch)* I really do need to speak to him! I need to make a move.
STACEY	Hang on. You can't just leave. What's going on?
LINDA	*(making to leave, then pausing to think and turning back towards Stacey)* Ok. I suppose you should know what's going on. But you'll need to come back at this time tomorrow.
STACEY	Why? What for?

LINDA Something needs sorting out, and I think you are involved.

STACEY What!?

LINDA *(exiting)* Please; come here tomorrow, at 12.

She exits

STACEY *(in disbelief)* What the… *(taking out her phone and heading off, pushing the pram. Into phone)* Shell…

She exits. Lights fade to black out

Scene 3

Day 4. 11:45am.
Linda and Ian are sat on the bench. We join them midway through a slightly heated discussion.

LINDA	I said I'm sorry.
IAN	I know. It's just that Charles had decided to let things lie and now it's all going to get messy.
LINDA	I didn't know that she'd given the money, or at least some of it, back. Did I?
IAN	No, you didn't.
LINDA	So, I thought I was helping out. I just thought of the first thing I could to get her to come back here.
IAN	I know. It's just that saying midday, here, means she might come at the same time as Charles.
LINDA	I'm sorry. I don't know what I was thinking.
IAN	No.
LINDA	For all we know, she might not come at all. I probably wasn't very convincing.
IAN	Or she comes with the police.
LINDA	What; having been the thief in the first place!?
IAN	But Charles has most of the money back and we don't have any evidence.
LINDA	I don't think she'll bring the police.
IAN	Maybe not.
LINDA	No.
IAN	She might just bring all her ex-boyfriends instead!
LINDA	How do you know she has lots of ex-boyfriends?

IAN		When she was explaining the baby's name.
LINDA		Named after one, was he?
IAN		No. That's the point. He's not.
LINDA		Oh.
IAN		Although she insisted on naming them all… All the ex-boyfriends… Dave Dee, Dozy, Beaky, Mick and Titch.
LINDA		*(laughing)* Surely not!?
IAN		*(smiling)* Well, no. But it was something like that. I can't remember.
LINDA		No, well, I'm not surprised you can't remember. You had enough difficulty trying to remember Jim. Didn't you!?
IAN		True.

Charles enters carrying his cloth bag

CHARLES Ian. Linda. How wonderful seeing you both. Together!

Linda and Ian both rise

IAN *(shaking Charles' hand)* Good to see you, Charles.

LINDA *(also shaking Charles' hand)* Hello, again.

CHARLES Hello. *(Pause)* I'm getting the feeling this meeting isn't a pleasurable accident.

IAN Well; it sort of is and isn't.

CHARLES That's not particularly a clear answer, Ian. I've told you about being clear, haven't I!?

IAN *(sharing a smile with Linda)* Yes you have, Charles. Maybe we should all sit down.

Charles and Ian sit at each end of the bench

LINDA Room for a little one in the middle?

CHARLES *(moving slightly)* Absolutely, my dear.

Linda sits

LINDA A rose between two thorns, eh?

IAN *(smiling)* Quite!

CHARLES Ah. Perfect!

IAN What is?

CHARLES That phrase. 'A rose between two thorns'. You see, I don't know if I said that my wife's name was Rose.

IAN Oh, right. No, you didn't.

CHARLES And whenever anyone said that phrase; 'a rose between two thorns', she'd say that she, as a rose, only needed the one thorn. Me. *(He takes a hanky and dabs his eyes)*

LINDA Oh. How sweet.

CHARLES *(returning his hanky to his pocket)* Yes. I think it was meant to be sweet, although I was probably more of a thorn in her side.

LINDA Surely not.

CHARLES I guess we'll never know. *(Pause)* Anyway; this "is or isn't a pleasurable accident". Would you like to expand on that, Ian?

IAN Yes, well, a bit complicated…

CHARLES Oh, dear. What have you done now, Ian?

IAN What, me? Erm, no, not me this time.

CHARLES Oh.

LINDA No, it's me this time.

CHARLES   Oh. Right.

LINDA   I met Ian for lunch, yesterday.

CHARLES   Yes. Ian mentioned it.

LINDA   But, on my way to meeting him, I bumped into the girl with the pram.

CHARLES   Jim's mother?

LINDA   Yes. Just here, by this bench.

CHARLES   Right.

LINDA   At this point I obviously had no idea that she'd returned the money to you.

CHARLES   Well; it was just sat here by the bench. We assumed it was her.

LINDA   Yes, well, I had no idea and, well, one thing led to another and I asked her to come here at midday today.

CHARLES   For what purpose?

LINDA   To discuss your missing money.

CHARLES   Oh.

LINDA   I didn't know you'd got most of it back. I didn't know you wanted to leave things alone, and not challenge the girl, and I didn't know you were going to be here. It's such a mess and all I wanted to do was help you, Charles.

CHARLES   *(taking a moment)* It's alright my dear. It's quite clear your intentions were all honourable.

LINDA   They were. They are.

CHARLES   The question now is what to do.

Pause

IAN Leave.

CHARLES I beg your pardon.

IAN Just leave.

CHARLES I'm sorry, Ian. I don't follow.

IAN Just go away. From here. If she turns up, and no one's here, that's the end of it.

LINDA Hardly.

CHARLES Linda's right, Ian. It wouldn't really be the end of it. It would just be delaying things. And you know what happens if you delay things...

IAN *(sheepishly)* Yes.

CHARLES Therefore; I think we should just play things by ear. See what the girl has to say and react accordingly. If we're honest, and upfront, we can hopefully bring this all to a positive conclusion.

IAN If you think that's best, Charles.

CHARLES I do.

LINDA Ok.

Stacey enters slowly. Pushing the pram. Linda rises

LINDA Hello, again.

STACEY 'llo.

LINDA Thank you for coming to see us.

IAN Hello.

Stacey manages a slight smile towards Ian

STACEY Look; what's this all about. *(Pointing at Charles)* And who's he?

CHARLES *(rising and offering his hand)* Good afternoon. I'm Charles.

Taking a step back, refusing the hand shake

STACEY Right. So, what's this all about.

Linda, who is still standing, gestures to Charles to retake his seat. He does

LINDA Look, it's a bit delicate...

STACEY *(interrupting)* Are any of you the police?

LINDA No.

IAN What!? No.

CHARLES Absolutely not, my dear.

STACEY Good. In that case, then, I'm guessing you're after this.

She reaches under the blankets at the foot of the pram and pulls out the plastic bag of money. She holds the bag towards Ian

Yours, right?

IAN *(shaking his head)* Wrong. *(Pointing towards Charles)* His.

STACEY What!?

CHARLES True. I left it here, by accident, obviously, after talking to Ian.

IAN *(at Stacey)* Then I spoke to you and left.

CHARLES And we assume you then found the bag and believed it to belong to Ian.

STACEY Yeh. I guess that probably makes sense.

IAN	But Linda didn't know that you'd returned most of the money yesterday when she asked you to come along today. If she had known, then this awkward little meeting wouldn't have had to take place.
LINDA	*(smiling)* Sorry!
STACEY	*(looking confused)* What do you mean "returned most of the money yesterday"?
CHARLES	The bag that was here, yesterday, when I came to meet Ian.
STACEY	I'm sorry. I have no idea what you're talking about.
IAN	The bag. You left a bag here, for me, although it was really for Charles.
STACEY	What!?
IAN	You guessed I'd be here for lunch. Left the bag. Walked past to check I'd got it...

Stacey looks completely dumbfounded

	No?
STACEY	No.
LINDA	You didn't leave a bag of money here, yesterday?
STACEY	No! This is the money. Take it!

She thrusts it at Ian. He takes it and just stares at it

CHARLES	*(looking at the bag)* That's definitely the same bag I left here. Then what was the bag that was here yesterday?
STACEY	What bag?
CHARLES	The bag of money that we thought you'd left... It was the same as this. I'm getting a trifle confused.
STACEY	You're not the only one!

IAN	Show her, Charles.
CHARLES	Sorry?
IAN	Show her.
CHARLES	Show her what?
IAN	The bag! The bag of money!
CHARLES	Oh, I see. I'm afraid I don't have that with me.
IAN	Don't have it… Where is it then?
CHARLES	At home.
IAN	At home!?
CHARLES	Yes. In its designated place.
IAN	Ah… Right.
LINDA	Hang on. Before we discuss the other bag, shall we discuss this one?
IAN	What do you mean?
LINDA	*(at Stacey)* I'm sorry, but we don't know your name.
STACEY	Erm…
LINDA	It's ok. You're not in trouble. We have the money back.

Pause

STACEY	It's Stacey.
LINDA	Hello, Stacey. I was just wondering what your plan was for this money, if I hadn't asked you to come here today?
STACEY	No idea. I wish I'd never picked it up.
LINDA	What do you mean?

STACEY Well, I thought I'd just hand it in to the police.

IAN Then why didn't you? Charles went there straight away.

STACEY Well, I called Shell…

LINDA Shell?

STACEY Yeh, my mate Shell. Shelley. She said not to go to the police as I'd get myself into trouble.

IAN More trouble than keeping the money?

STACEY She said the police would accuse me of nicking it.

CHARLES I think I'm getting confused again.

LINDA I don't think the police would.

STACEY It's not me, you see, but some of my ex-boyfriends haven't been – how shall I put it – the nicest guys.

LINDA Right.

STACEY So, Shell thought they might link the money to them and I don't want some of those guys resurfacing; if you know what I mean. Asking if they're Jim's dad. Asking for DNA tests. We're better off without them. Any of 'em. If you know what I mean.

LINDA I think so.

IAN So, once Shell put you off the police, what was your plan?

STACEY No idea. I thought about putting it into a savings account for Jim.

LINDA That's a nice idea.

STACEY But I didn't want his savings to be built on money which wasn't his in the first place. Not a good place to start.

LINDA   No.

STACEY   It might make him end up like his dad... Whoever that is...

Glances are shared

             Shell wanted me to spend it.

IAN   Which you did.

STACEY   Sorry?

IAN   You spent it. Well, some of it.

STACEY   *(raising her voice)* No I did not. It's all there. Every penny!

IAN   I thought we were £300 short.

CHARLES   That was the other money, Ian.

IAN   What? Oh, yes. I'm sorry, Stacey. *I'm* now getting confused.

STACEY   Well...

IAN   It's just... where did the new pram come from?

STACEY   What?

IAN   The new pram appeared just after the money disappeared and the other money was £300 short...

STACEY   So, *(pointing at the pram)* you thought I'd spent some money on this?

IAN   Yes. Sorry. It did sort of add up.

STACEY   *(chuckling)* Yes, well, I suppose it did.

IAN   Sorry.

STACEY It's ok. This pram is from my aunt who lives in Canada. She reserved it at the posh baby shop down the High Street. All I had to do was choose the colour when I collected it.

IAN Ah, right.

STACEY And, for your information, it was £400 not £300!

They all chuckle

Look. I'm sorry I took your money. I wish I hadn't. It's been a nightmare since I picked it up. I'm glad you've got it back.

CHARLES Well, Stacey, even though you should have handed it to the police; I'm glad you picked the money up.

STACEY Why?

CHARLES Well, someone else may have just spent it. But even though you found it a nightmare to have, you looked after it. Thank you.

Ian hands the bag to Charles

STACEY Aren't you gonna count it, then?

CHARLES No need. I trust you.

Stacey starts to well-up

Oh, dear. Have I said something wrong?

STACEY No. I'm sorry. It's just that I don't think anyone's ever said they trust me before.

CHARLES Ah, well. There's a first time for everything!

STACEY Thank you!

Pause

IAN The question still remains. Where did the bag of £700 come from?

LINDA	Good grief. I'd forgotten about that.
CHARLES	Maybe you'd like it, Stacey? Maybe open that savings account for Jim?
STACEY	That's very kind, but I'd still be opening an account with money which may have had a dodgy past.
CHARLES	True, true.
STACEY	Hang on. Did you say the bag of money was by this bench?
CHARLES	Yes, why?
STACEY	Well, you know I said some of my ex-boyfriends weren't the nicest guys.
CHARLES	Yes.
STACEY	Well some of them dealt in drugs and they sometimes used the park bins as drop-off points for drugs or cash.
CHARLES	Right.
STACEY	Maybe this bench is a new drop-off point.
CHARLES	Oh, dear. *(Looking at the far end of the bench)* You wouldn't like that, would you, Rose?

Ian and Linda look at where Charles is looking. Stacey stares at Charles

STACEY	You what!?
LINDA	*(quietly)* Don't worry. I'll explain, later.
STACEY	*(looking bemused)* Oh, ok.
IAN	So; if it's drugs money, what do we do? Hand it in to the police?
STACEY	No way. *(There's a stirring from the pram)* Oh, no. It looks like Jim's waking up. I'm going to get moving again.

Both Charles and Ian rise

IAN   Ok.

CHARLES   Right you are.

Stacey starts to leave

LINDA   Hang on, Stacey.

STACEY   What?

LINDA   I've got a bit of an idea. Can we walk and talk?

STACEY   *(heading off)* I guess so.

Linda and Stacey exit. Charles and Ian shrug at each other and follow them off. Charles is clutching his bag of money. We start to hear Linda mumbling her idea to Stacey as they exit the stage. Charles and Ian are leaning forward to listen in

Lights fade to black out

Scene 4

Day 5. 12:00pm.
Lights up on the park bench. Linda and Ian enter. Ian is looking shifty.
He has a bulge in his jacket which he's trying to hold in place. They sit
on the bench.

LINDA   Stop looking so shifty.

IAN   I'm not looking shifty.

LINDA   You are. And take your hand out of your jacket. You look like Nelson.

IAN   Nelson Mandela never used to hold his arm inside his jacket.

LINDA   Horatio Nelson!

IAN   Oh, right. *(Removing his hand)* Better?

LINDA   Yes.

IAN   Now what?

LINDA   Now we stick to the plan. Wait until anyone dodgy looking starts looking interested in the bench. Wait 'til they move away. Then pop the bag on the ground by the bench. Retreat to the bushes where Charles and Stacey are and see if the dodgy looking person returns for the bag.

IAN   Then, what?

LINDA   Take the video, which Stacey's going to take of them, to the police.

IAN   Will the police buy that?

LINDA   Well, they probably won't be able to use any video as evidence, but as Stacey says; the police know she has hung around with not the nicest guys and if we turn up with her, and the video, they'll see she's trying to do the right thing and turn over a new leaf.

IAN	Which I think she is.
LINDA	Yes. I think so, too.

Pause

IAN	How long are we going to do this?
LINDA	Do what?
IAN	This. Sit here and wait for someone dodgy looking to appear.
LINDA	Don't know.
IAN	Could be days.

Tina and Colin enter. Usual attire. Slightly behind the bench. Phones in the air etc. Ian and Linda catch sight of them

LINDA	*(sotto)* Act normal.
IAN	*(sotto)* Sorry?
LINDA	*(sotto)* Act normal!
IAN	*(sotto)* Oh, right.

Pause. Tina and Colin are taking photos etc. They clearly think that they haven't been spotted

LINDA	*(sotto)* Well, go on then
IAN	*(sotto)* What!?
LINDA	*(sotto)* Act normal!
IAN	*(sotto)* I am acting normal!
LINDA	*(sotto)* What!?
IAN	*(sotto)* We normally sit in silence. So, I'm acting normal!

LINDA   (deciding to take the lead. Slightly louder than necessary) Oh, look, darling. A pigeon.

IAN   (also louder than necessary and slightly wooden) Oh, yes, my dear. A pigeon. What a surprise to see a pigeon in a park!

LINDA   (glaring) No. Not really.

Linda continues to glare and thumps Ian on his leg, out of sight of the geocachers

IAN   (responding to the thump) Ah! (Trying to cover up) So you're right. I thought you said penguin.

Colin and Tina stop what they're doing and glare at Ian. Linda also glares. A moment, then Colin and Tina exit

LINDA   A penguin!?

IAN   Sorry. I panicked.

LINDA   Good grief! That was acting normal?

IAN   I'm sorry. I'm clearly not cut out for this.

LINDA   You're telling me!?

IAN   Sorry. (Pause) Do you think they were dodgy looking?

LINDA   Were *they* dodgy looking!? I think we were probably dodgy looking to them!

IAN   Possibly. But they did look interested in the bench.

LINDA   Yes. I suppose they did.

IAN   Yes.

LINDA   Although they didn't really look like drug dealers. Or gangsters.

IAN   Well, they certainly weren't carrying violin cases.

LINDA   You know what I mean.

IAN I know. I reckon they were in disguise.

LINDA Disguise.

IAN Yep. Ramblers rambling around the park.

LINDA Shall we put the bag down and see if they come back?

IAN Can do. Where are they now?

LINDA *(pointing)* Over there. By that other bench.

IAN Looks like they're definitely looking for something by a bench. I'm going for it!

Ian swiftly places the bag by the leg of the bench

LINDA Let's join Charles and Stacey in the bushes.

They both exit. Pause

Colin and Tina enter. They sit on the bench without noticing the bag

COLIN Did you see him. The boss man.

TINA Yes.

COLIN Bold as brass. Talking about money with his new jezebel.

TINA New! She looked anything but new.

COLIN Obviously one for the older, more discerning gentleman.

TINA Yes. *(Pause)* What do you mean, discussing money?

COLIN Didn't you hear them? Pigeons and Penguins.

TINA Yes. What about them?

COLIN Slang, isn't it. For money.

TINA Is it?

COLIN	Yes. You know. Pony, Monkey, Pigeon, Penguin. Different amounts of money.
TINA	Really?
COLIN	Oh, yes.
TINA	How much are they all worth?
COLIN	Absolutely no idea!
TINA	Ah!
COLIN	Anyway. A few more bits of evidence and then we can approach the police.
TINA	You sure?
COLIN	Oh, yes.
TINA	All seems a bit vague to me…
COLIN	Not at all. We'll soon have them bang to rights.
TINA	*(unconvinced)* Mmm…
COLIN	Right. What's for lunch?
TINA	*(opening her bag and removing a coolbag)* Pork pies followed by millionaire's shortbread.
COLIN	Ooo… porky pies. My favourite. *(Taking the bag)* Let me take that from you.
TINA	Thank you.
COLIN	*(placing the bag by his feet and noticing the plastic bag)* Hello. What's this?
TINA	What's what?
COLIN	*(picking up the bag)* This bag.
TINA	Oh my God! The boss man has left it to do another transaction. We've ended up in the middle of it!

COLIN		This looks like the plastic bag we left the other day.
TINA		It's just a plastic bag, Colin. Just leave it and let's go.
COLIN		*(opening the bag)* Hang on. I want to take a look.
TINA		Don't!
COLIN		As you said; it's just a plastic bag.
TINA		Yes. But… be careful.
COLIN		*(slowly removing the envelope of cash)* It is the bag we left the other day.
TINA		How do you know?
COLIN		*(removing a £20 note)* It's the same money.
TINA		How do you know?
COLIN		Because it's fake.
TINA		I thought it's meant to be a really good fake.
COLIN		Oh, it is, but I've had it long enough to spot the error.
TINA		Really? What's that, then?
COLIN		*(holding the note up)* The Queen's got a squint.
TINA		*(not looking at the note)* No she hasn't.
COLIN		On the note, Tina. On the note!
TINA		*(looking at the note)* Oh, right. So she has.

Colin and Tina study the note which Colin is holding up whilst Charles, Stacey, Linda and Ian quietly walk across behind the bench without being seen. Linda is pushing the pram whilst Stacey is filming Colin and Tina. Ian is on the phone. They exit

Now what?

COLIN Well. It looks like the boss man hasn't spotted the squint.

TINA No.

COLIN Not surprising really.

TINA What do you mean?

COLIN Well. Drugs dealer. Not going to be a royalist. Is he!?

TINA I suppose not!

COLIN So, our money has entered the web of lies…

TINA Sorry!?

COLIN Our money has entered the web…

TINA *(interrupting)* Yes. I heard what you said! What do you mean!?

COLIN Well… it means we're in… doesn't it?

TINA Does it?

COLIN *(vaguely)* Yes.

TINA You have no idea what you're talking about. Do you?

COLIN *(slumping)* No.

TINA Great.

COLIN *(recovering slightly)* Well. We could let the police know that if any fake cash appears on the scene it's come from dodgy people.

TINA *(pointing at the note Colin's still holding)* Yes. You. Your fingerprints will be all over it.

COLIN *(rubbing the note on his sleeve and replacing it in the envelope)* Crikey!

TINA I don't know, Colin. I think we're out of our depth. We should just take the money home.

COLIN Take it home!

TINA And burn it.

COLIN Take it home and burn it! We can't do that.

TINA Why not?

COLIN Why not!?! Because it's no longer ours. It's been put here for someone else.

TINA So why are we fiddling with it?

COLIN Fair point.

TINA Put it back on the floor and let's go.

COLIN Ok.

Colin starts to lean down to replace the bag when the voice of a police officer is heard from off-stage, via a loud hailer

POLICE *(off)* Stand up and put your hands in the air!

COLIN *(springing up and holding his hands up. The plastic bag still in one hand)* Ahh!

TINA *(looking at Colin)* What are you doing?

COLIN Following instructions. *(Pointing off)* Can't you see him?

TINA Yes. I can see him, but we've done nothing wrong.

POLICE *(off)* I said stand up and put your hands in the air.

COLIN *(frantically)* I am! I am!

POLICE *(off)* Not you. The other one.

COLIN Stand up, Tina.

TINA   But we've done nothing wrong. *(Shouting towards the police)* We've done nothing wrong!

POLICE   *(off)* Stand up. Raise your hands. We're armed.

TINA   *(raising her voice)* No you're not. Unless a loud hailer is considered a weapon?

POLICE   *(off. Slightly exasperated)* Not me; Dave.

TINA   Dave?

POLICE   *(off)* Yes. Dave. He's on his way from the car with a taser. So we are armed. Or, at least, he is.

TINA   *(slowly standing up and raising her hands)* Well. If Dave's on his way with a taser, I'll comply.

POLICE   *(off)* And Geoff.

TINA   Geoff?

POLICE   *(off)* Yes. Geoff's heading here right now with Sheba.

TINA   Oh, they sound a lovely couple.

COLIN   *(still quivering with his hands in the air. Sotto)* What are you doing!?

POLICE   *(off)* Sheba's his dog. His police dog.

TINA   Ok. Ok. You can stop, now. You had me with taser.

POLICE   *(off)* Now, slowly walk towards me. Keep your hands up and bring the drugs and money with you.

COLIN   Drugs? No. No drugs. Just money.

POLICE   *(off)* Bring the money, then.

COLIN   But it's fake.

TINA   *(sotto)* Brilliant. That's really gonna help!

COLIN   The Queen has a squint.

POLICE   *(off)* Her Majesty did not have a squint!

COLIN   No. I know she didn't actually have a squint, but she does on the fake money. *(Reaching into the bag)* Let me show you.

POLICE   *(off)* Do not put your hand in the bag. If you do, Dave will taser you.

COLIN   *(removing his hand)* No. Don't!

TINA   *(sotto)* I wish he would.

Colin glares at Tina

POLICE   *(off)* Now slowly walk towards me. No funny business.

Colin and Tina slowly exit

               Cuff him, Danno.

TINA   *(off)* Is his name really Danno?

POLICE   *(off. No longer through the loud hailer. Sheepishly)* No.

TINA   *(off)* Thought not.

Lights fade to black out

Scene 5

A few days later. Around midday.
Linda and Ian are sat on the bench. Linda in the middle, Ian at 'Rose's' end. There's a space for Charles at his end. Stacey is stood behind the pram next to Ian's end of the bench. They are currently involved in small talk.

IAN *(rising)* Here he is!

Charles enters

CHARLES *(waving Ian down)* Don't get up on my account, Ian.

Ian sits. Charles sits in the space at his usual end of the bench

Lovely to see you all.

LINDA Hello Charles.

STACEY *(smiling)* Hi.

CHARLES Any news about the; what were they? Geo… geo…

LINDA Geocachers, Charles.

CHARLES Yes. Them. Whatever that is.

IAN Well. It looks like they've just been given a warning for not handing in the fake money when they were supposed to have done; after they found it in a geocache some time ago.

CHARLES Right.

LINDA And they've been told to bring any suspicions they have of people to them and not turn detective themselves.

CHARLES Yes. Well. We did a bit of that ourselves, didn't we!?

IAN Yes.

LINDA But Stacey's got some good news; haven't you Stacey?

STACEY   Yes. I got a £50 shop voucher for help in the community. For helping the police track down fake money.

CHARLES   Well, that's wonderful.

LINDA   And we bought the voucher off Stacey so she could have cash instead and… *(looking at Stacey)*

STACEY   *(getting the drift)* …and I put it into a savings account for Jim!

CHARLES   Ah. That is wonderful.

Pause

LINDA   Right. We're off to lunch, aren't we?

IAN   Yes.

CHARLES   Lovely.

LINDA   But we have a gift for you.

CHARLES   For me?

LINDA   Yes.

Linda stands and moves towards Stacey. Behind her, on the back of the bench, is a brass plaque inscribed 'Rose and Charles. Our bench.'

CHARLES   *(immediately welling up)* Oh, my. *(Reading the plaque)* 'Rose and Charles. Our bench.' That's wonderful!

LINDA   Are you sure?

CHARLES   *(fetching his hanky and dabbing his eyes)* Oh, yes.

LINDA   You don't think we've defaced your bench or anything, do you?

CHARLES   Oh, no.

IAN   Good.

CHARLES Mind you, it would be a bit too late if I did!

IAN Not really. *(Pulling the plaque off)* It's only stuck on with double-sided sticky tape!

CHARLES Oh.

LINDA Oh, Ian. We just wanted to make sure you were happy with it before attaching it properly.

CHARLES Oh, I see. Very thoughtful.

Ian sticks the plaque back on

LINDA If you're 100% certain, the council will fix it properly.

CHARLES That's wonderful. Thank you, all.

STACEY Jim's waking up. I better start another circuit.

LINDA Can we walk with you for a bit?

STACEY Of course. *(Looking into the pram. Addressing Jim)* Say "come on Auntie Linda. Come on Uncle Ian"!

Linda and Ian smile at this and follow Stacey off

LINDA Bye, Charles.

IAN Bye.

CHARLES Goodbye and thank you again.

IAN You're welcome. See you soon.

STACEY *(off)* Bye.

CHARLES Bye, Stacey.

Pause

Charles stares at the plaque and dabs his eyes a few times

Well. That was all a bit of an adventure. Just because I hadn't got round to designating a place for the money.

He removes the plaque and looks at it

> And now I shall designate a place for you, until the council are ready to put you permanently on the bench. *(Smiling at the plaque)* Our bench.

He rises. Gives the back of the bench a little tap as he exits

Lights fade to black out

The End

Printed in Great Britain
by Amazon